THE ESSENTIAL COLLECTION

CHOPIN

GOLD

T0061482

Published by
Chester Music Limited
14-15 Berners Street, London W1T 3LJ, UK.

Exclusive Distributors:
Music Sales Limited
Distribution Centre, Newmarket Road, Bury St Edmunds, Suffolk IP33 3YB, UK.
Music Sales Corporation
180 Madison Avenue, 24th Floor, New York NY 10016, USA.
Music Sales Pty Limited
4th floor, Lisgar House, 30-32 Carrington Street, Sydney, NSW 2000, Australia.

Order No. CH80124R
ISBN 978-1-78558-041-3
This book © Copyright 2012 by Chester Music.

Audio Project Manager: Ruth Power.
Audio recorded and produced by Mutual Chord Studio, Guangzhou, China.

Previously published as Book Only Edition CH65681.

Book printed and Audio manufactured in the EU.

Your Guarantee of Quality:
As publishers, we strive to produce every book to the highest commercial standards.
The music has been carefully designed to minimise awkward page turns
and to make playing from it a real pleasure.
Particular care has been given to specifying acid-free, neutral-sized
paper made from pulps which have not been elemental chlorine bleached.
This pulp is from farmed sustainable forests and was produced
with special regard for the environment.
Throughout, the printing and binding have been planned to ensure a sturdy,
attractive publication which should give years of enjoyment.
If your copy fails to meet our high standards, please inform us and we will gladly replace it.

www.musicsales.com

CHESTER MUSIC
part of The Music Sales Group

London / New York / Paris / Sydney / Copenhagen / Berlin / Madrid / Hong Kong / Tokyo

Ballade No.1 in G minor, Op.23

Composed by Frédéric Chopin   Arranged by Jerry Lanning

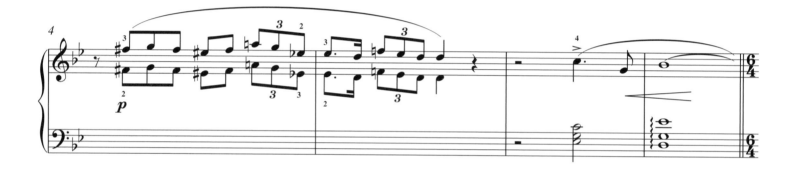

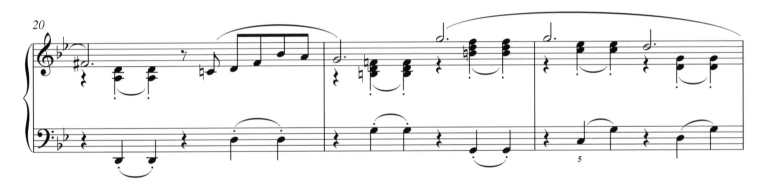

Meno mosso ($\quad$ = 120)

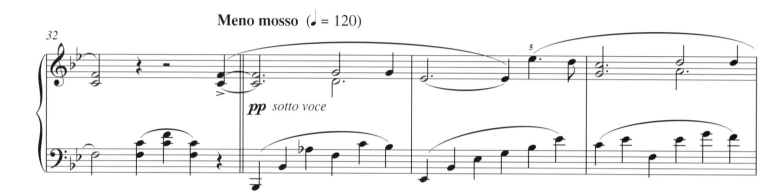

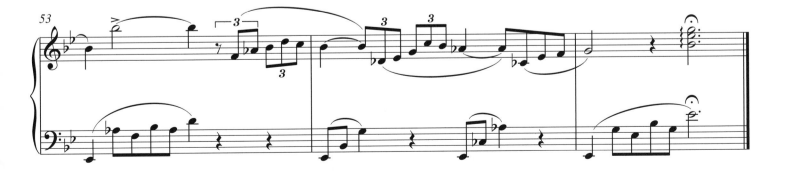

Cantabile in B♭ major

Composed by Frédéric Chopin   Arranged by Jerry Lanning

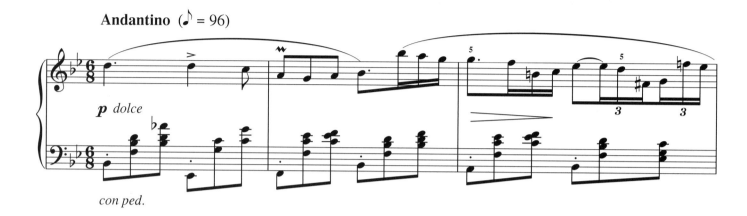

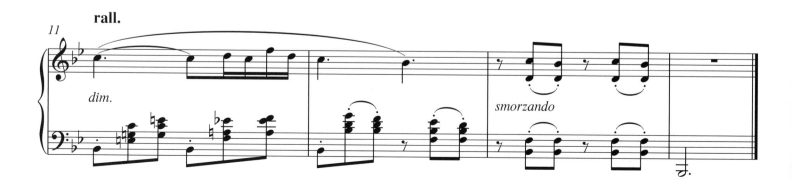

Étude in E major, Op.10, No.3

Composed by Frédéric Chopin   Arranged by Jerry Lanning

Lento ma non troppo (♪ = 68)

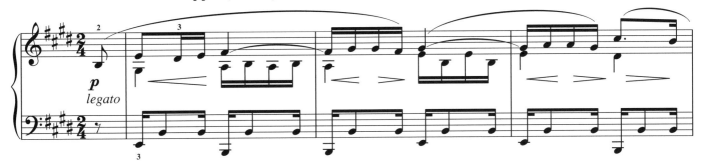

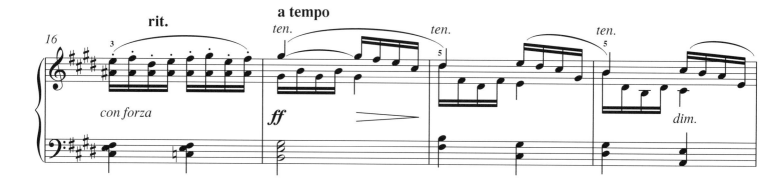

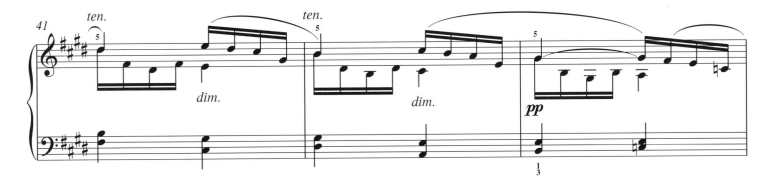

Impromptu No.4 in C♯ minor
'Fantaisie-Impromptu', Op.66

(Largo section)

Composed by Frédéric Chopin

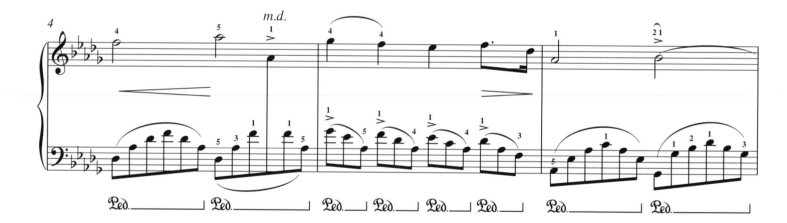

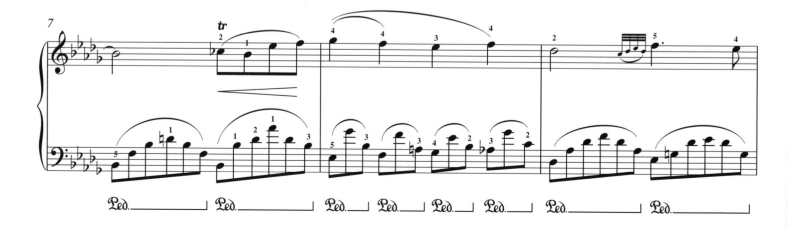

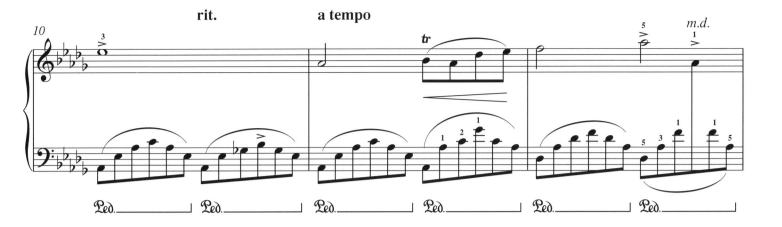

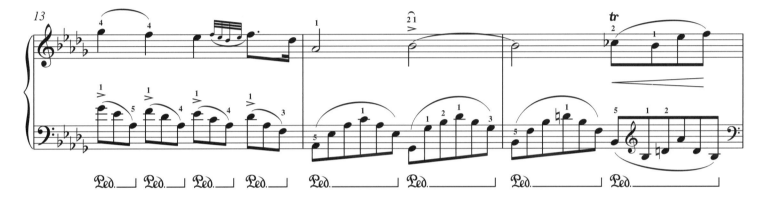

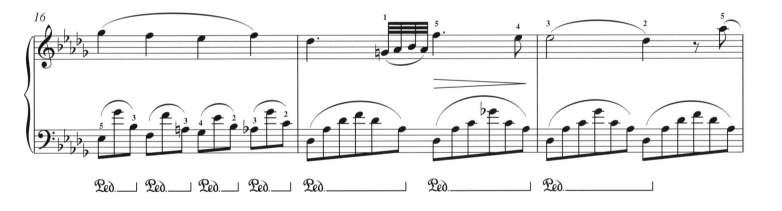

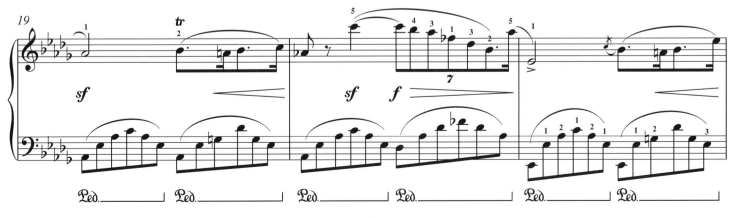

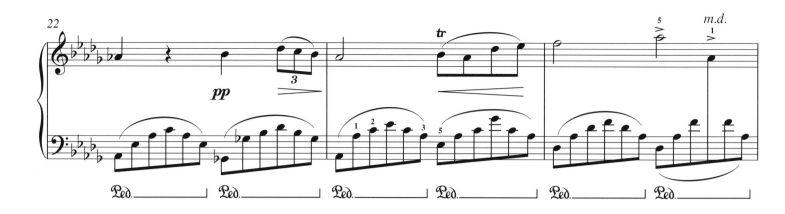

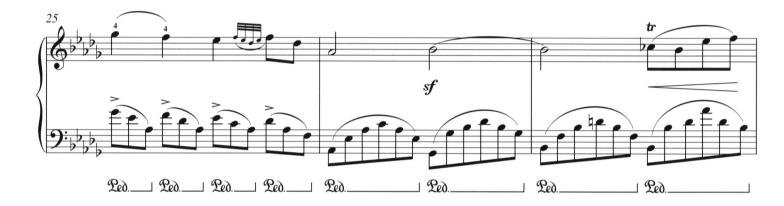

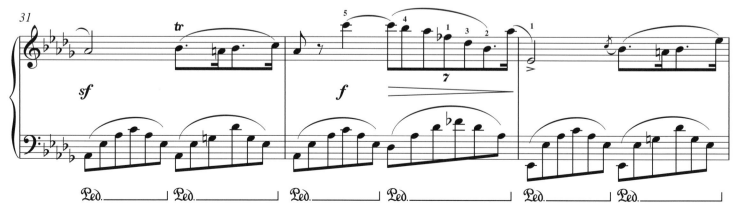

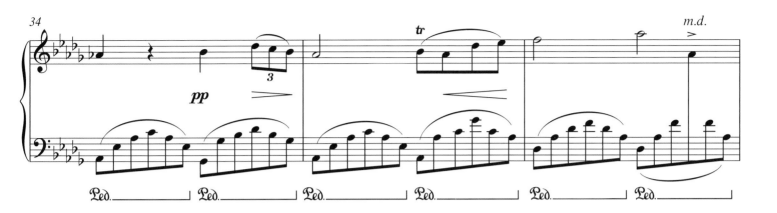

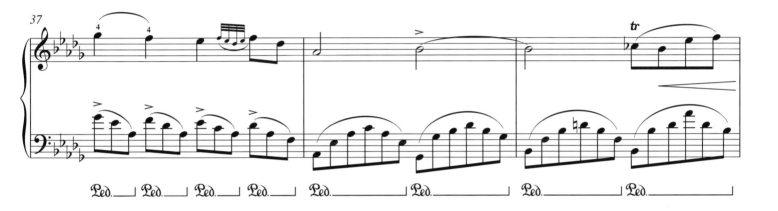

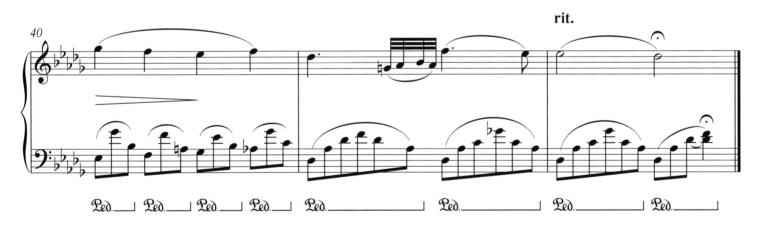

Largo in E♭ major, Op.posth.

Composed by Frédéric Chopin   Arranged by Jerry Lanning

Largo (♩ = 72)

Mazurka in B♭ major, Op.7, No.1

Composed by Frédéric Chopin

Vivace (♩. = 50)

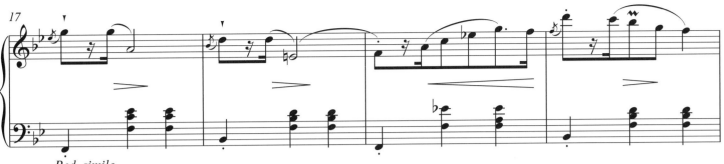

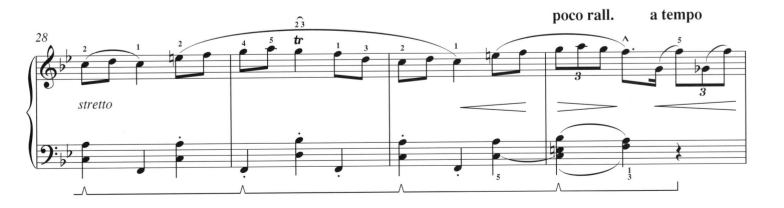

Mazurka in C major, Op.7, No.5

Composed by Frédéric Chopin

Mazurka in A minor, Op.68, No.2

Composed by Frédéric Chopin

poco a poco rit.

Tempo I

Mazurka in F major, Op.68, No.3

Composed by Frédéric Chopin

Allegretto, ma non troppo (♩ = 132)

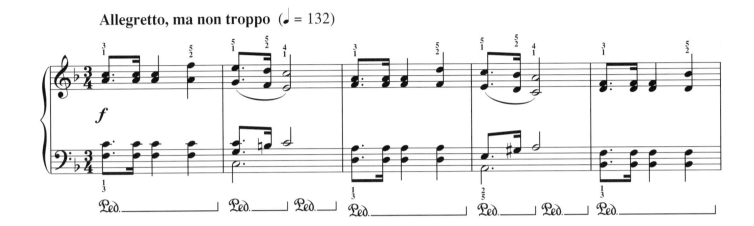

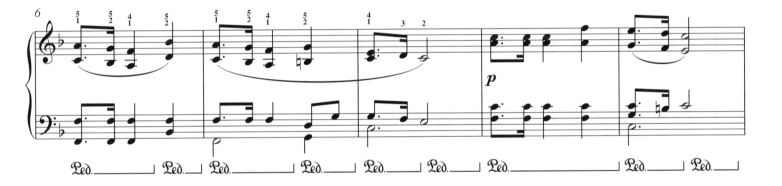

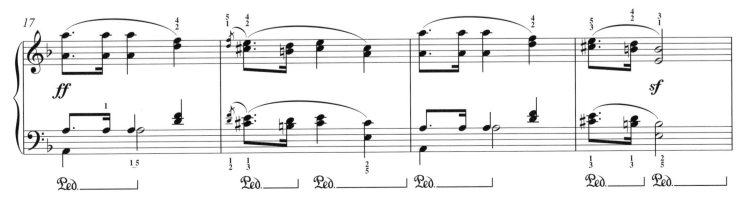

Poco più vivo

Ped. ten. _____

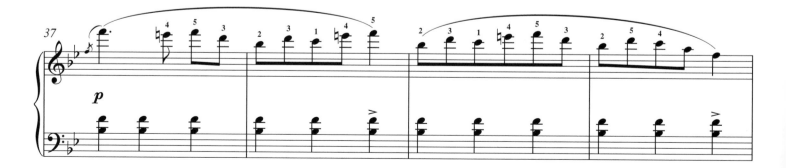

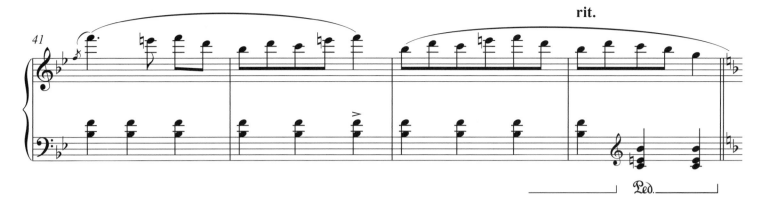

Tempo I

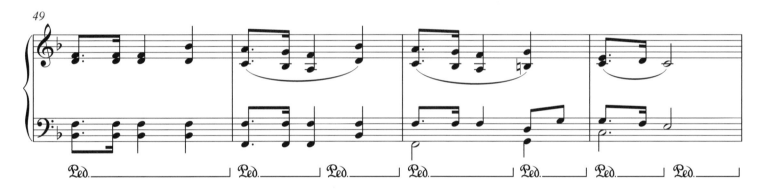

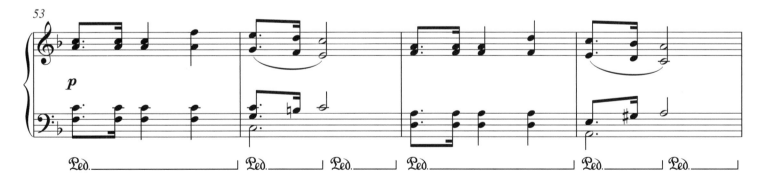

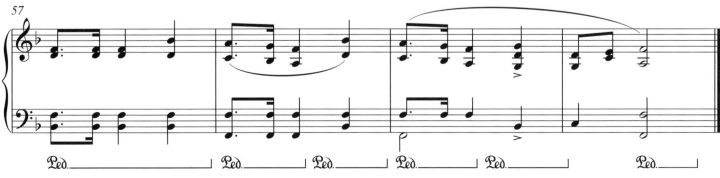

Nocturne in E♭ major, Op.9, No.2

Composed by Frédéric Chopin

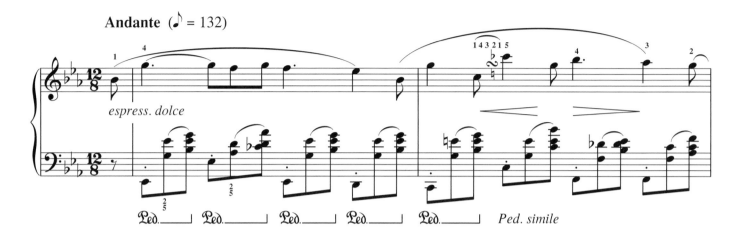

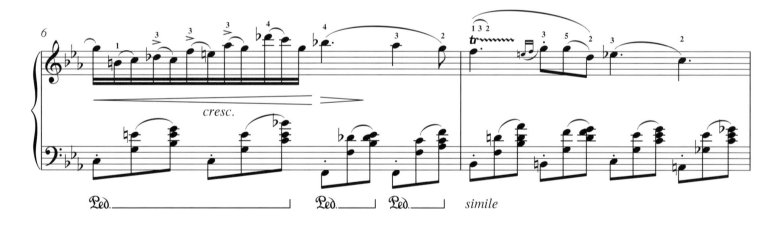

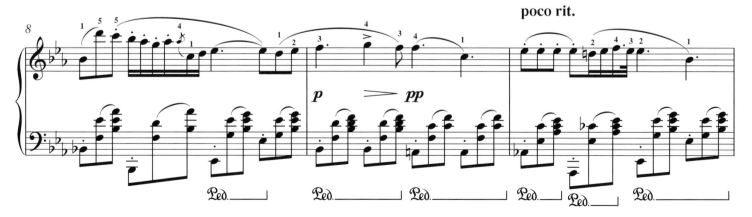

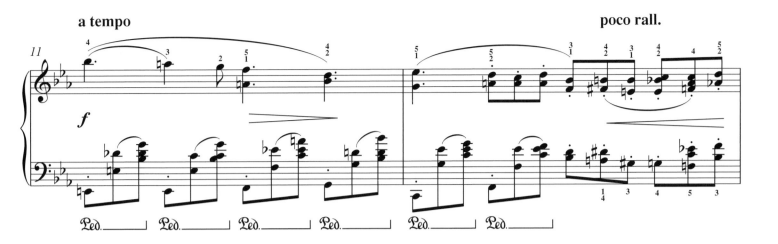

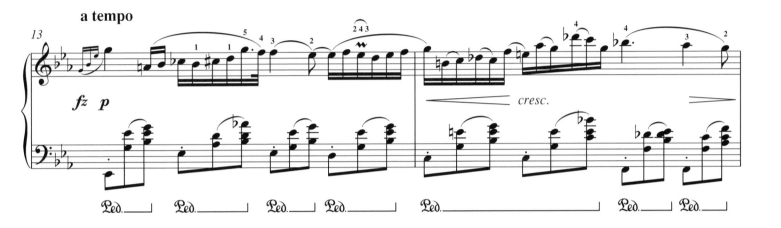

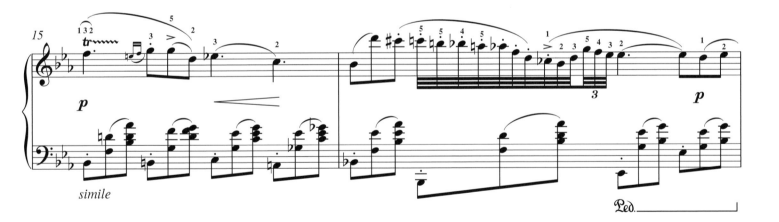

poco rall.   a tempo

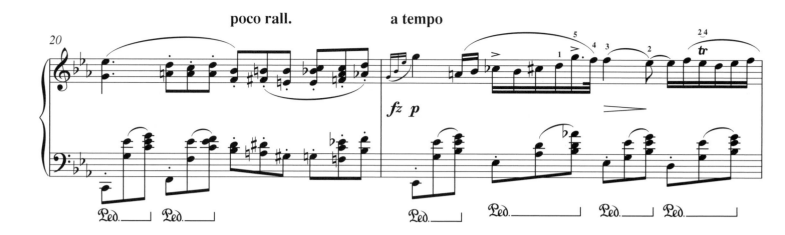

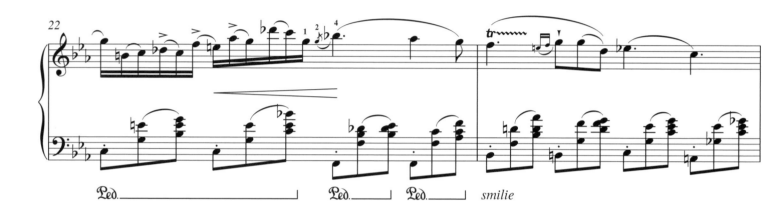

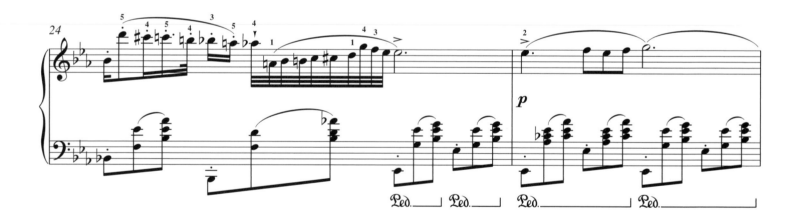

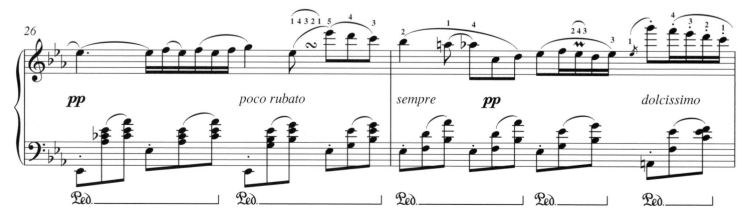

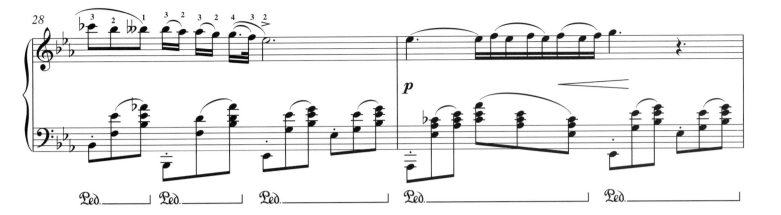

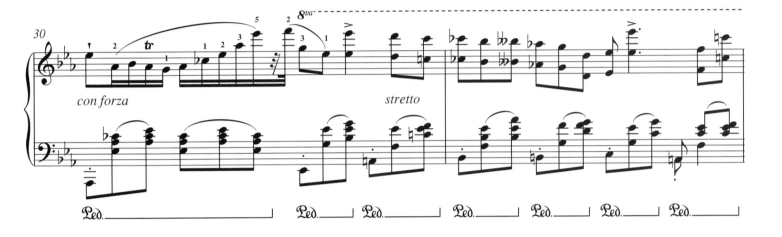

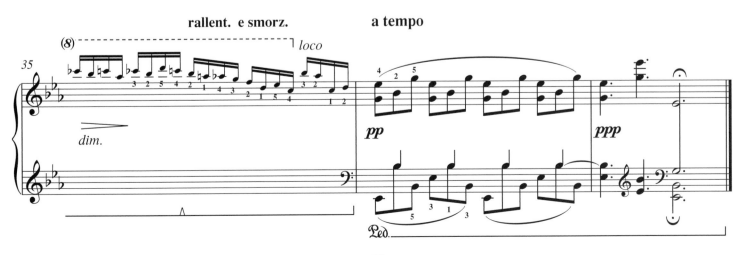

Nocturne in G minor, Op.15, No.3

Composed by Frédéric Chopin

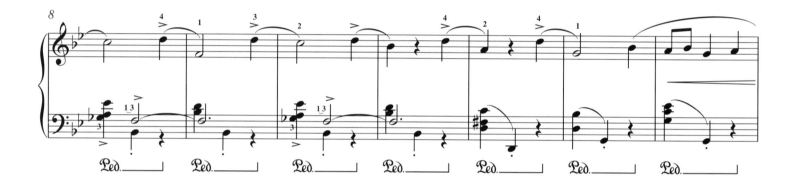

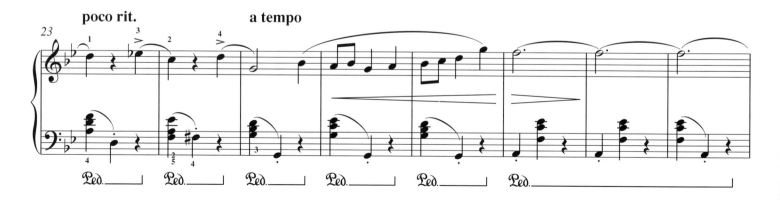

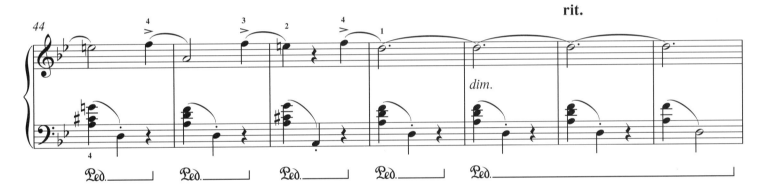

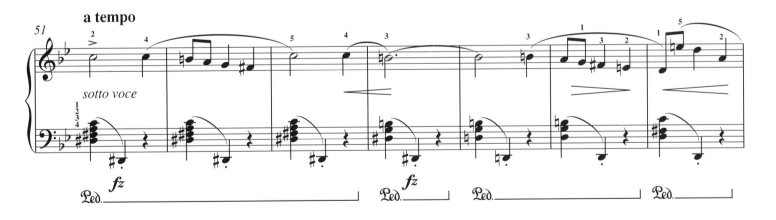

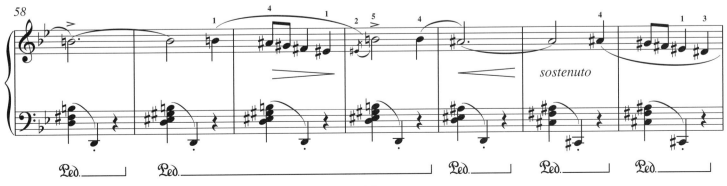

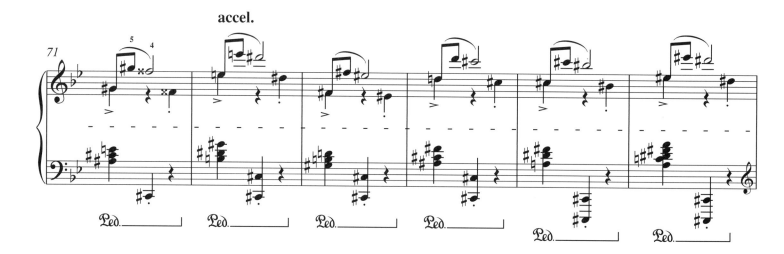

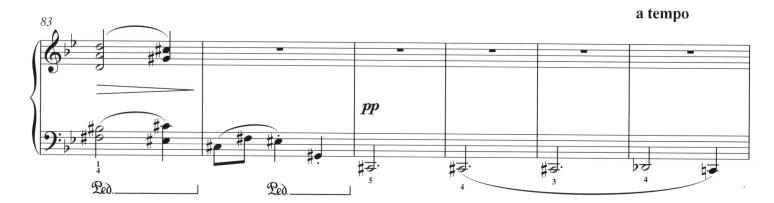

Religioso

p
sotto voce

sempre legato (con ped.)

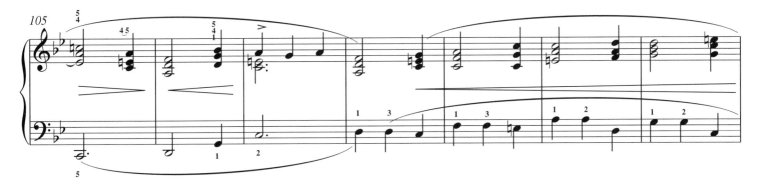

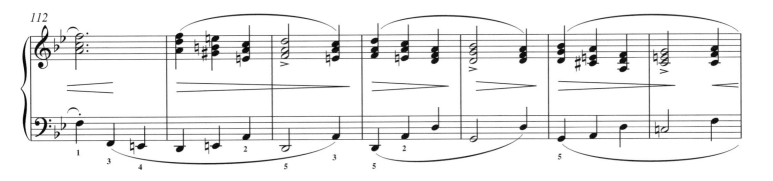

fz

fz

fz

fz

Ped.⎯⎯⎯⎯⎯⎯⎯

Ped.⎯⎯⎯⎯⎯⎯⎯

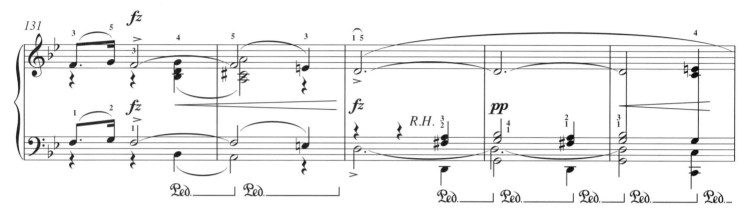

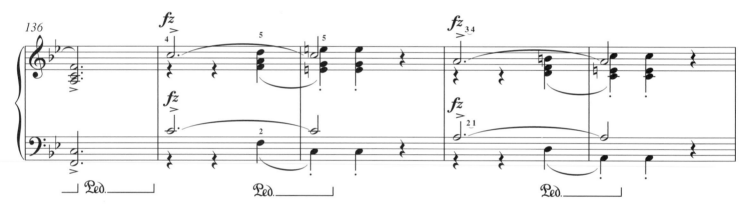

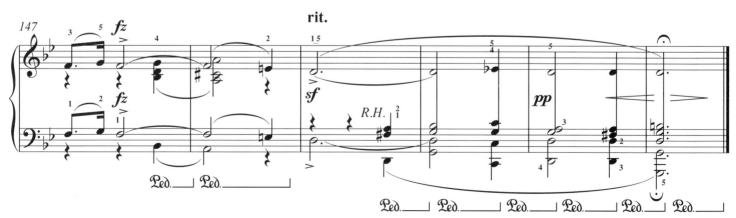

Nocturne in C♯ minor, Op.posth.

Composed by Frédéric Chopin   Arranged by Jerry Lanning

Lento con gran espressione (♩ = 68)

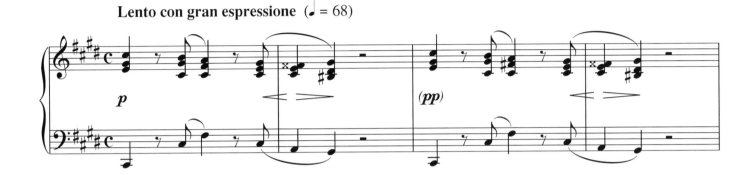

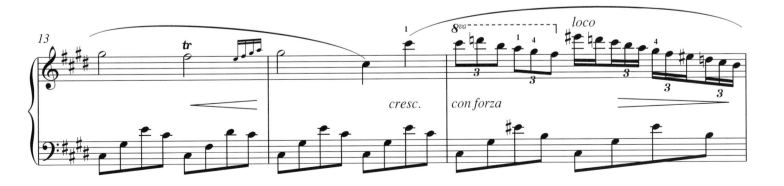

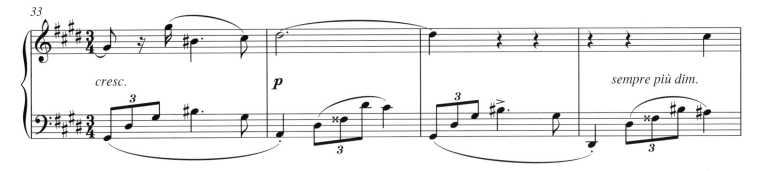

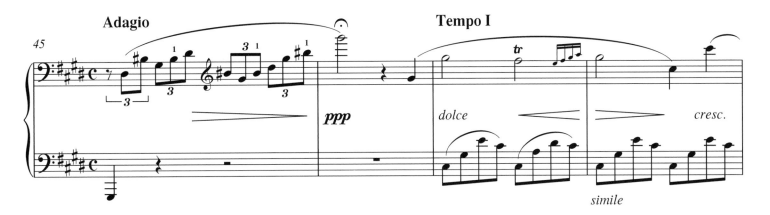

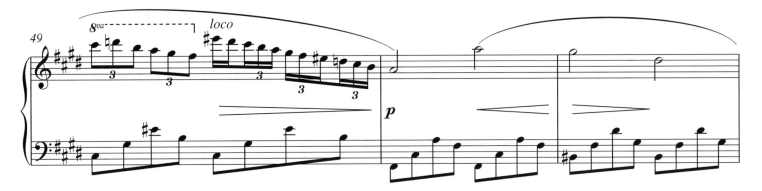

Nocturne in F minor, Op.55, No.1

Composed by Frédéric Chopin   Arranged by Jack Long

a tempo

rit.　　　　a tempo

Piano Concerto No.1 in E minor, Op.11
(2nd Movement: Romance)

Composed by Frédéric Chopin   Arranged by Jerry Lanning

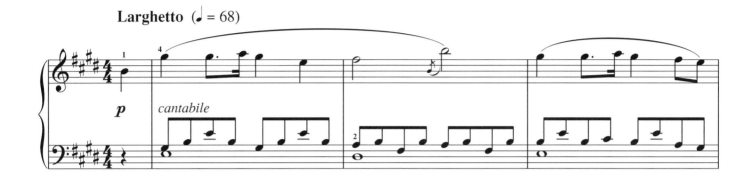

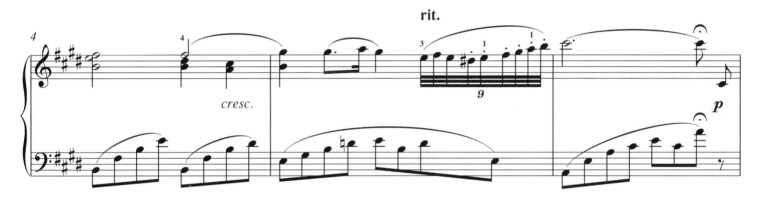

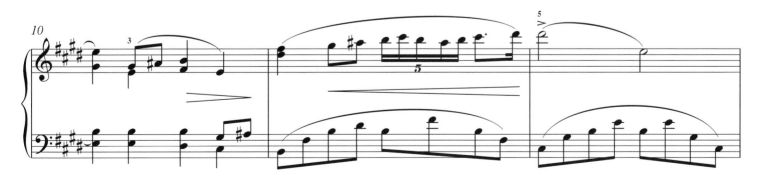

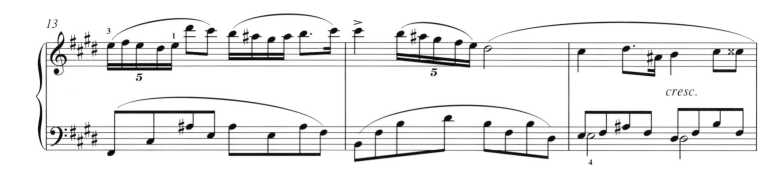

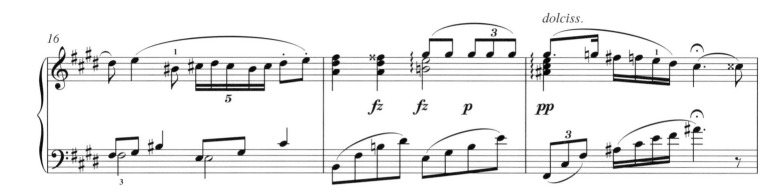

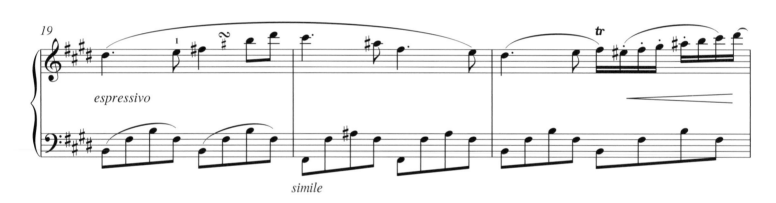

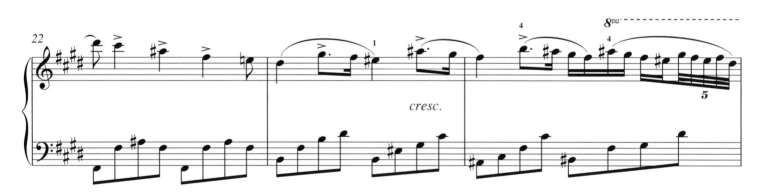

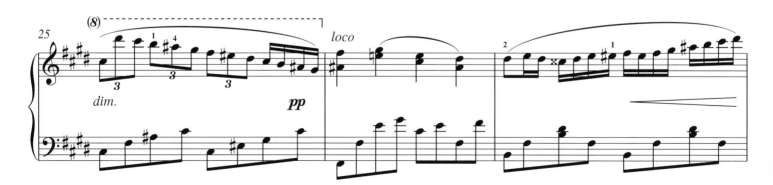

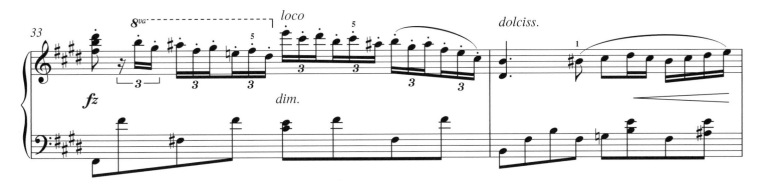

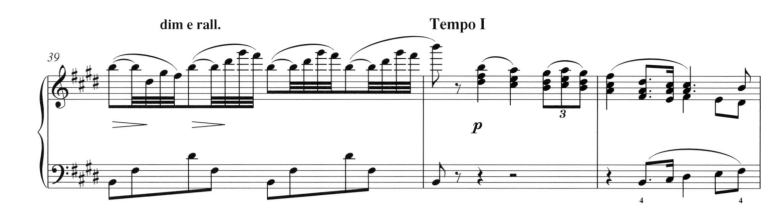

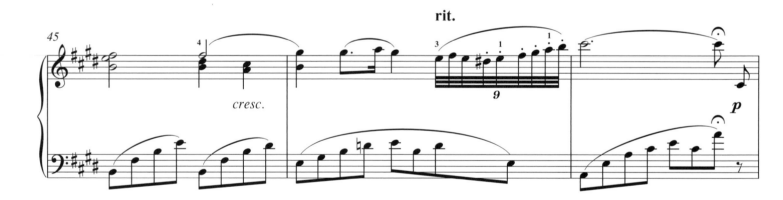

Polonaise in A major 'Militaire', Op.40, No.1

Composed by Frédéric Chopin   Arranged by Jerry Lanning

Allegro con brio (♩ = 92)

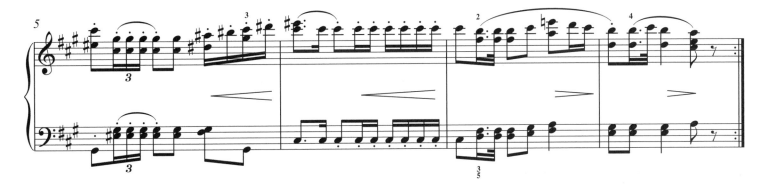

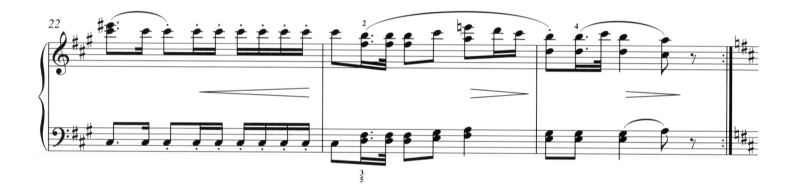

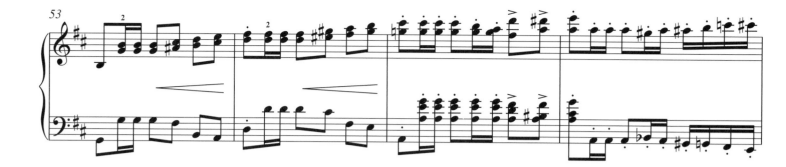

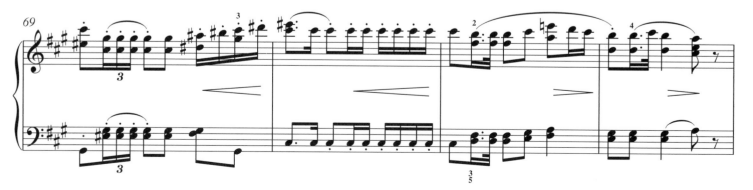

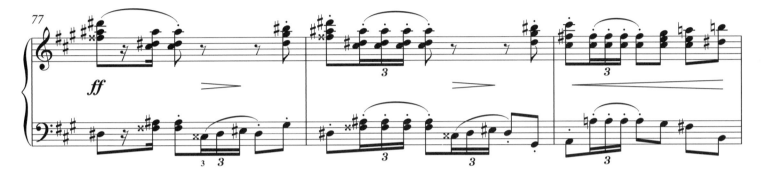

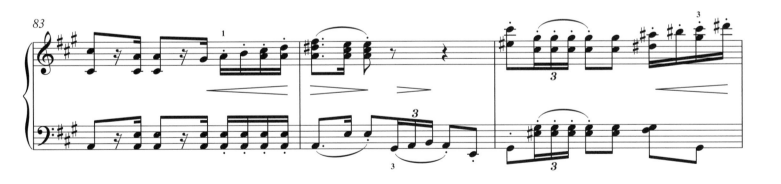

Prélude in E minor, Op.28, No.4

Composed by Frédéric Chopin

Largo

p   *espressivo*

tenuto sempre

poco rall.

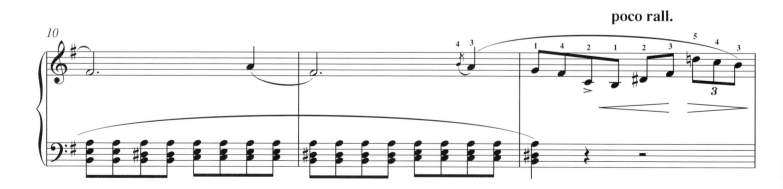

a tempo

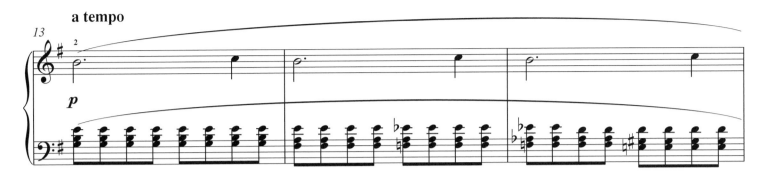

stretto

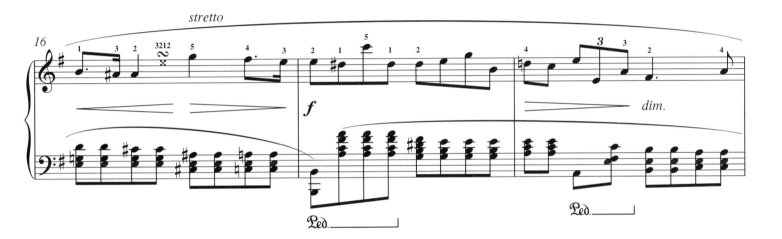

smorz.

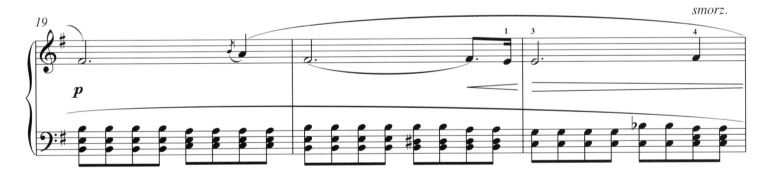

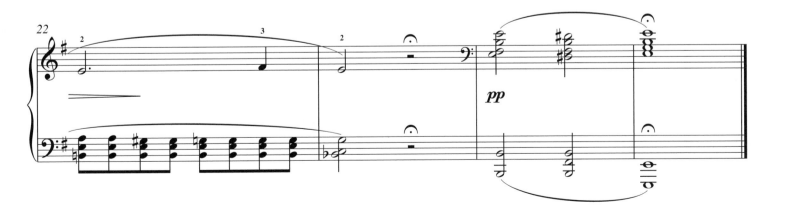

Prélude in A major, Op.28, No.7

Composed by Frédéric Chopin

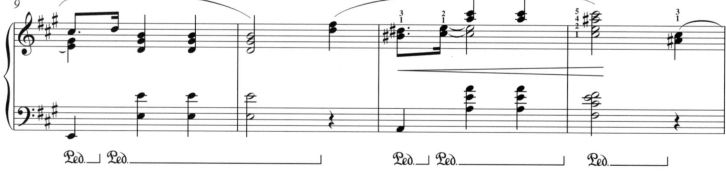

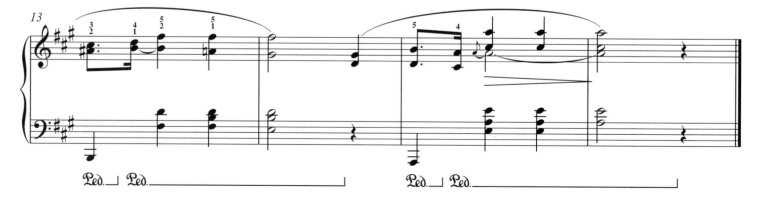

Prélude in Db major 'Raindrop', Op.28, No.15

Composed by Frédéric Chopin   Arranged by Jack Long

Andante sostenuto

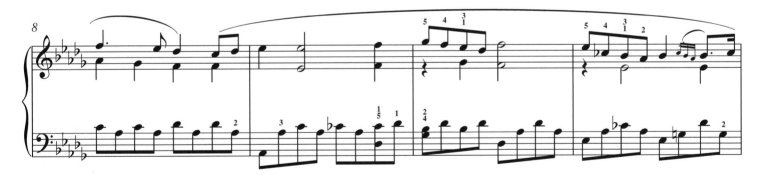

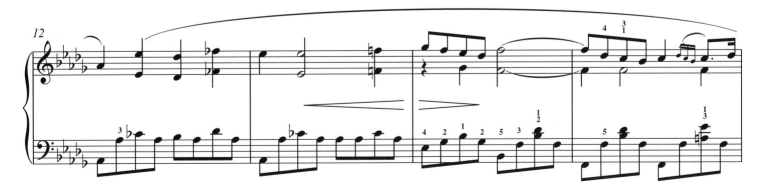

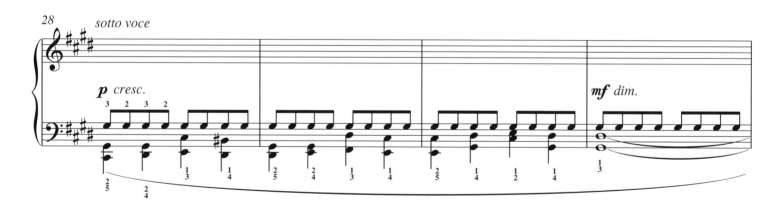

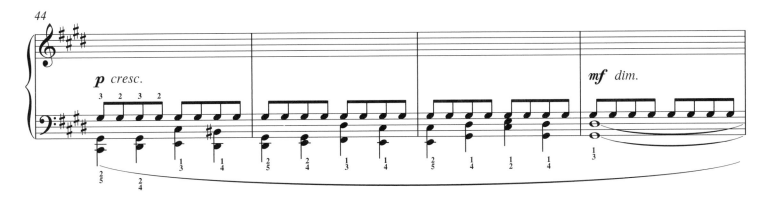

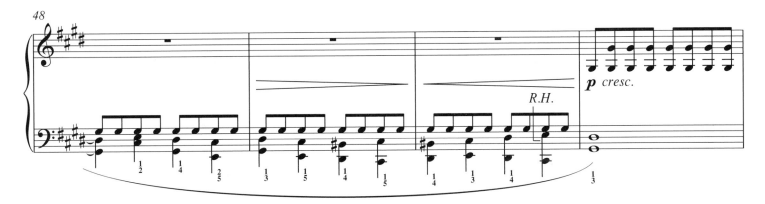

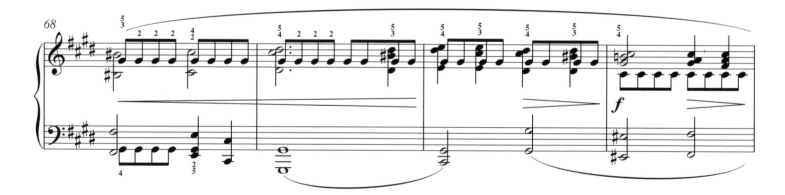

dim. e rit.

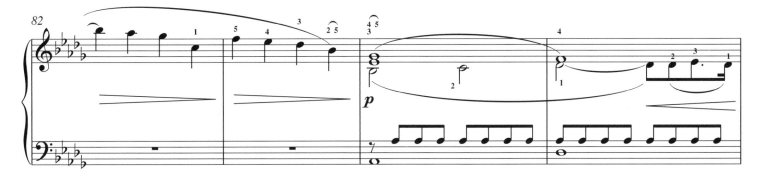

Prélude in C minor, Op.28, No.20

Composed by Frédéric Chopin

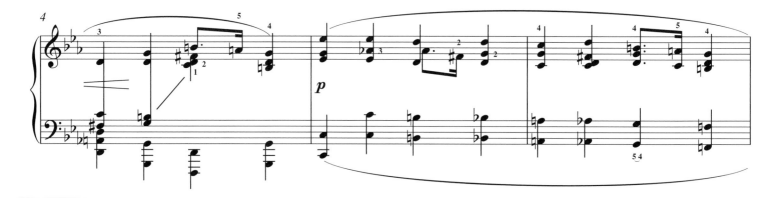

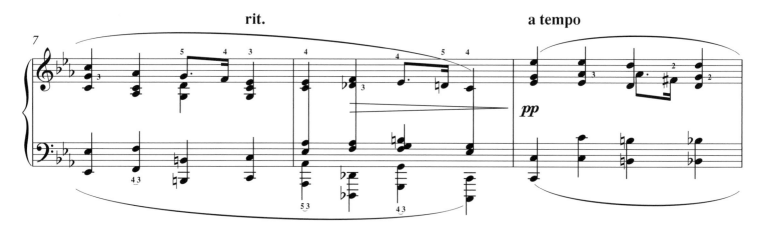

Prélude in B♭ major, Op.28, No.21

Composed by Frédéric Chopin

Cantabile

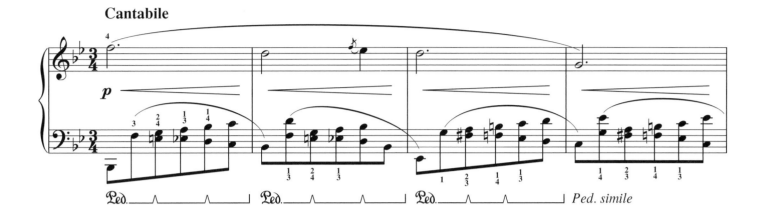

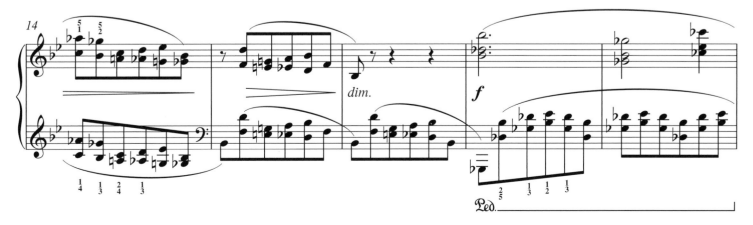

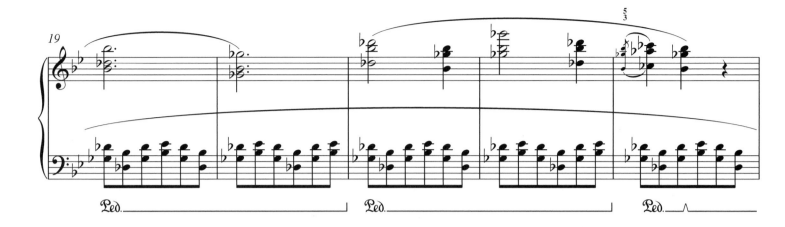

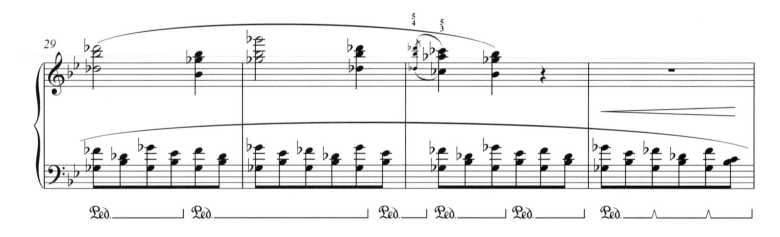

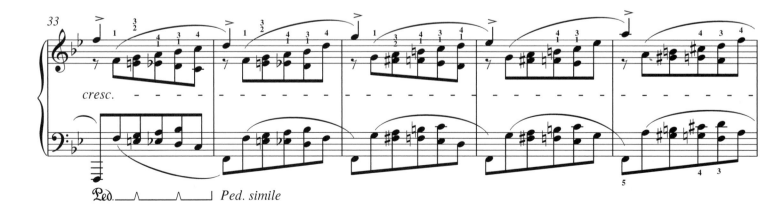

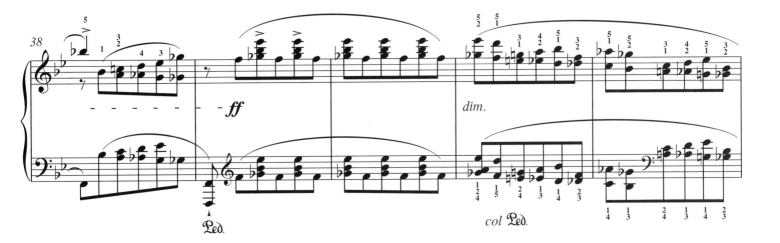

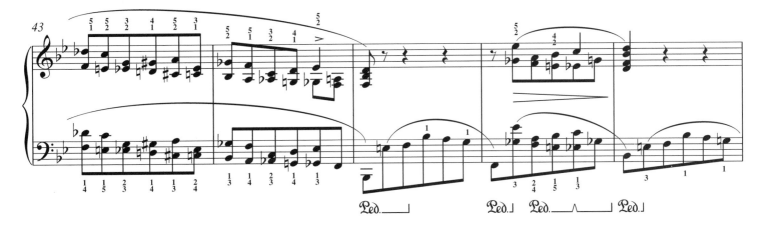

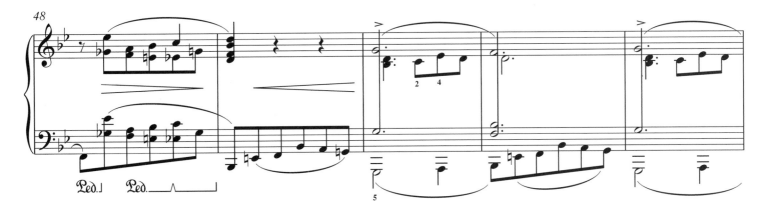

Sonata No.1 in C minor, Op.4

(2nd Movement: Menuetto and Trio)

Composed by Frédéric Chopin

Menuetto

Allegretto (♩. = 60)

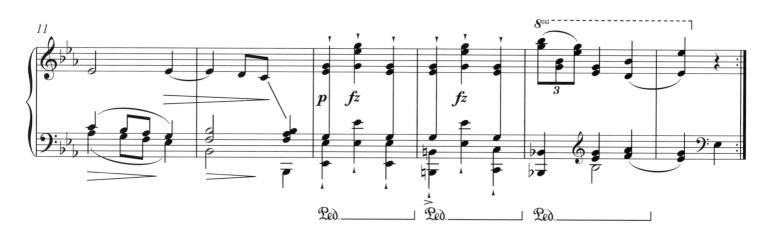

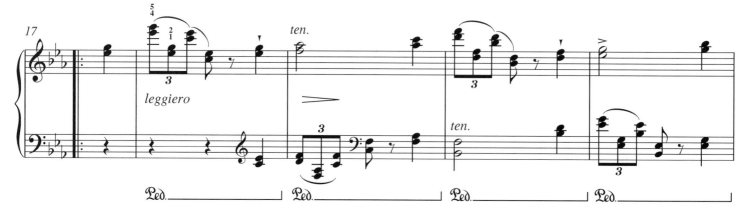

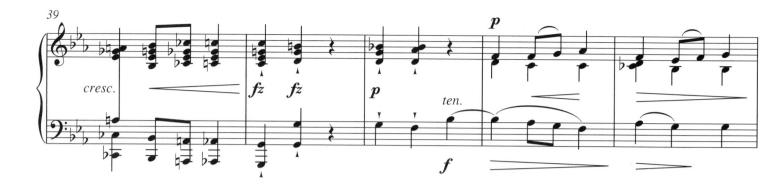

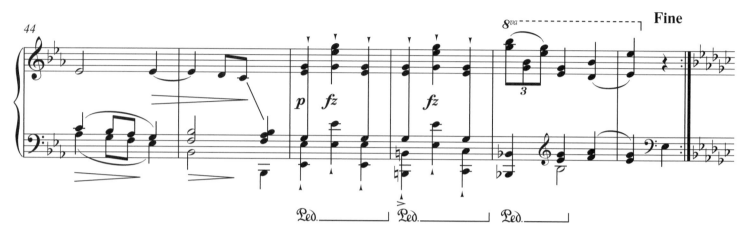

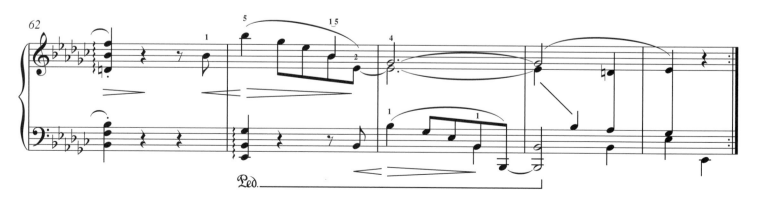

**Menuetto da Capo,
senza repetizione**

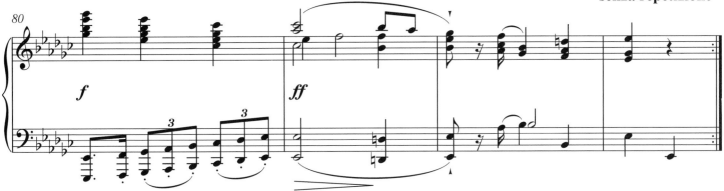

Sonata No.2 in B♭ minor 'Marche funèbre', Op.35

(3rd Movement: Lento)

Composed by Frédéric Chopin

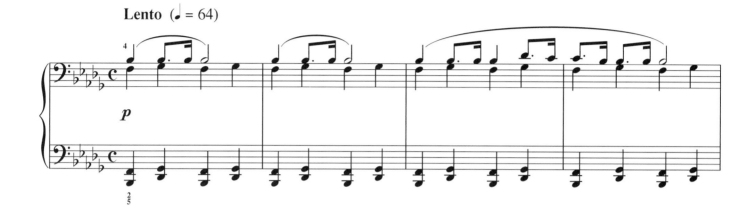

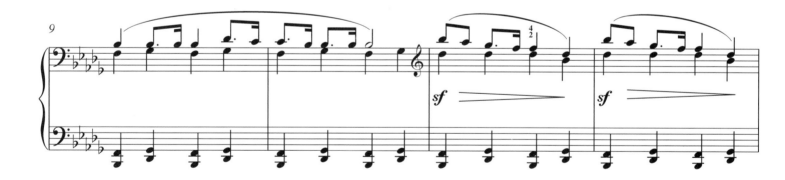

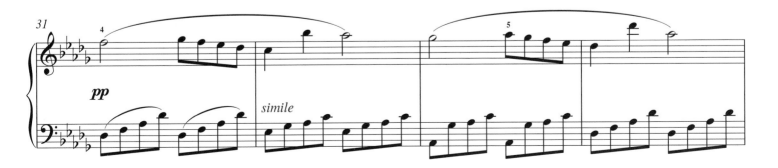

cresc. poco a poco

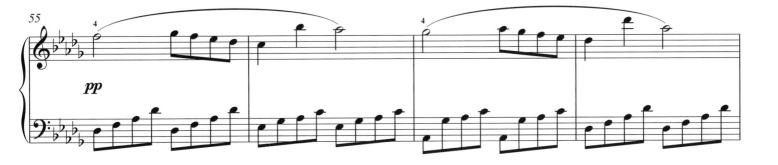

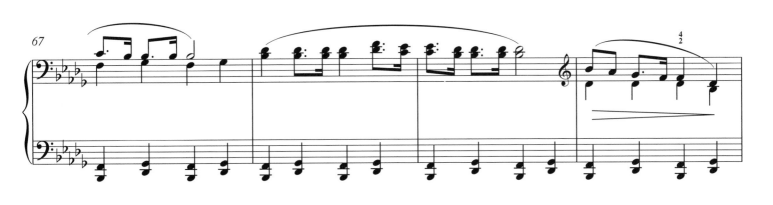

Valse in A minor 'Brillante', Op.34, No.2

Composed by Frédéric Chopin

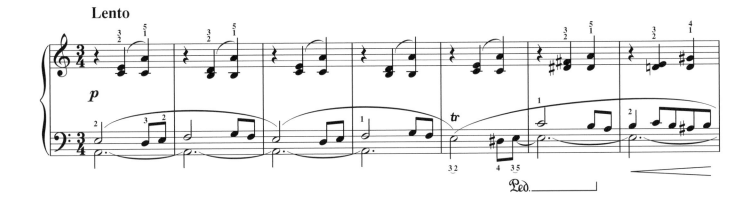

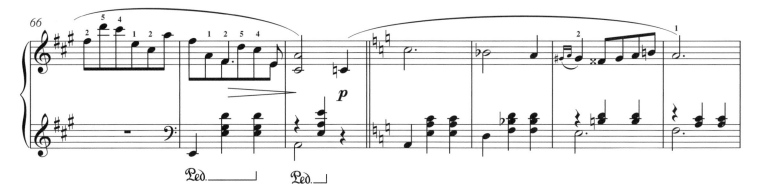

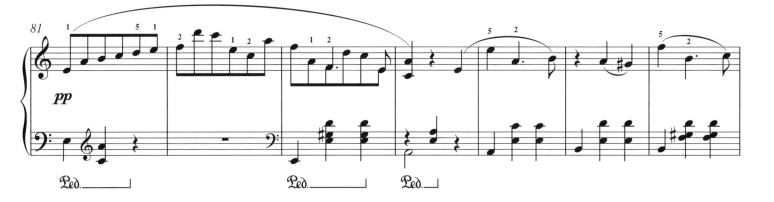

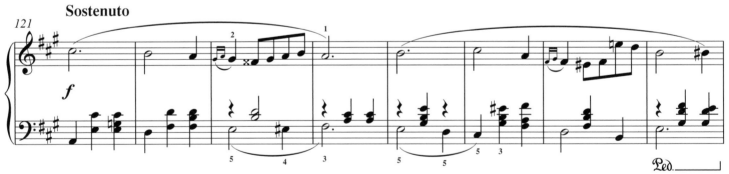

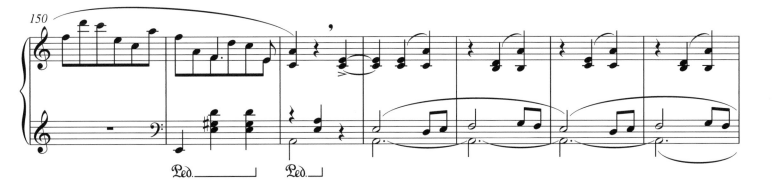

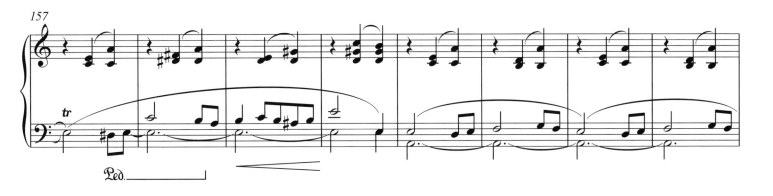

Poco più mosso

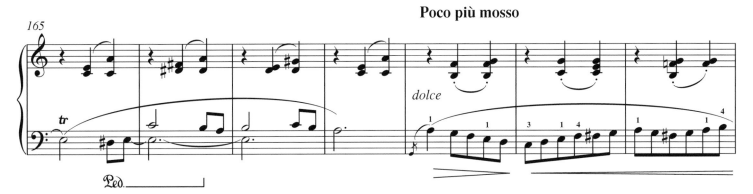

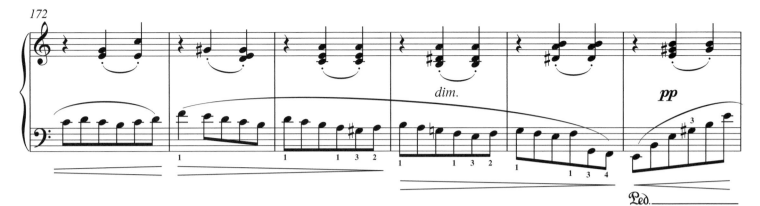

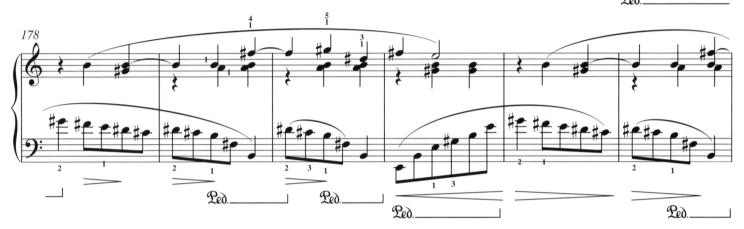

poco rit.   a tempo primo

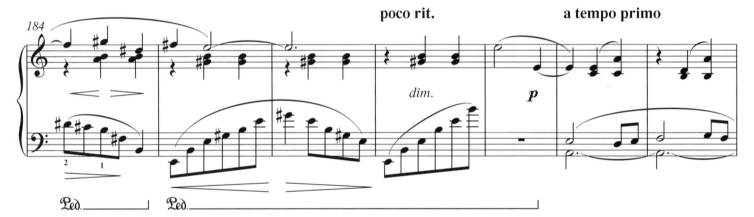

Valse in D♭ major 'Minute Waltz', Op.64, No.1

Composed by Frédéric Chopin

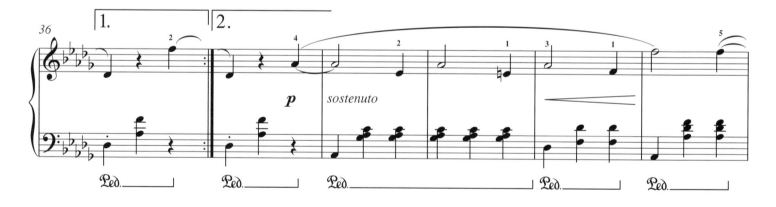

82

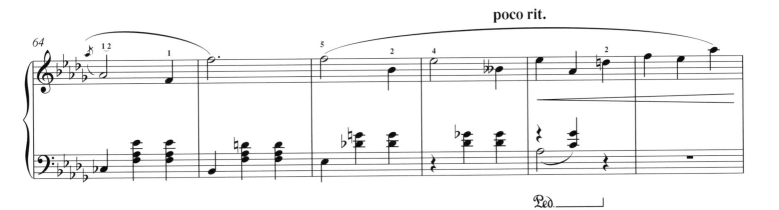

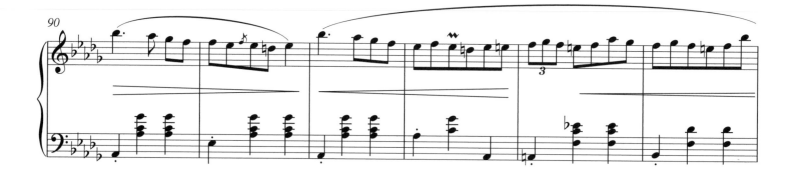

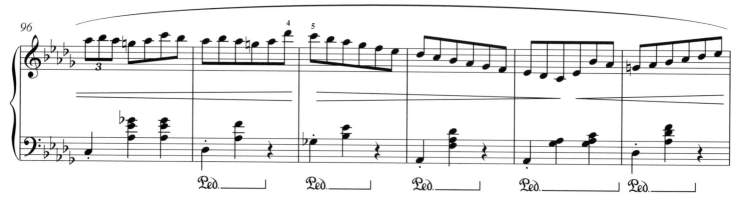

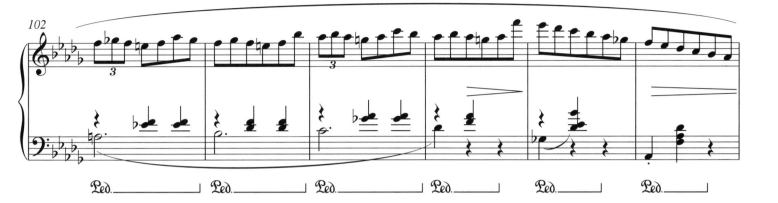

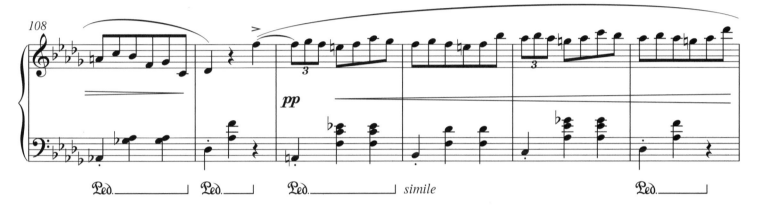

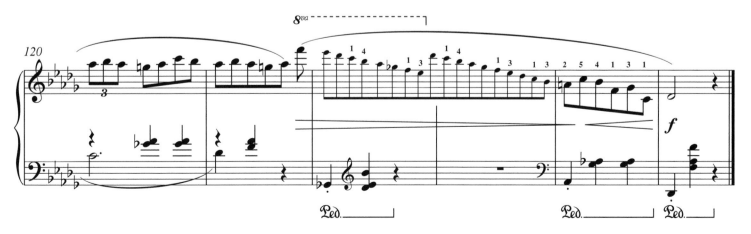

Valse in A♭ major, Op.69, No.1

(Posthumous)

Composed by Frédéric Chopin

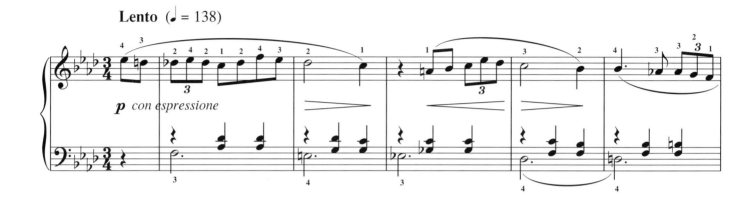

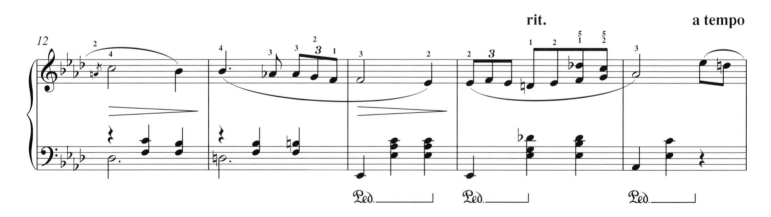

rit.   a tempo

Con anima

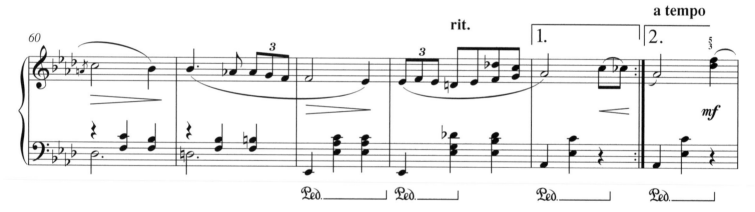

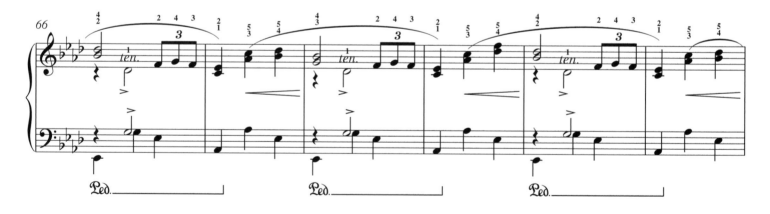

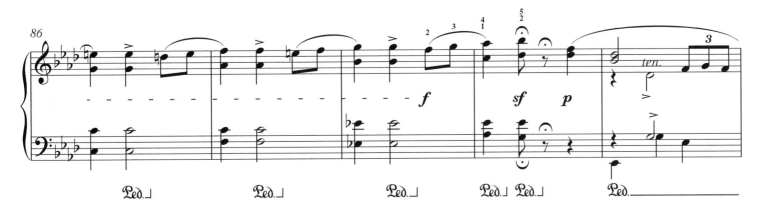

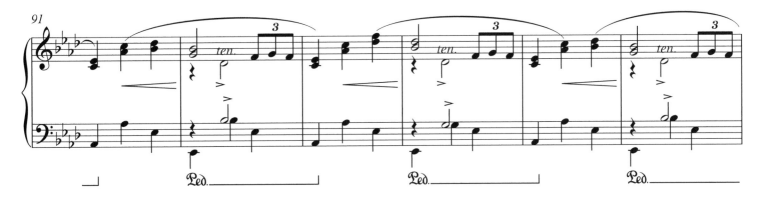

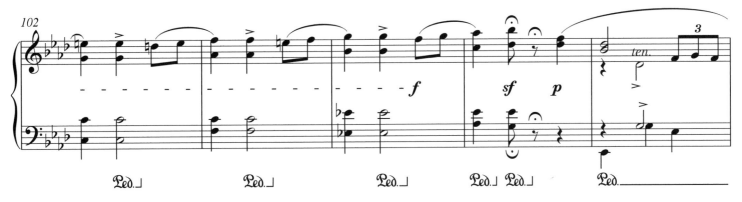

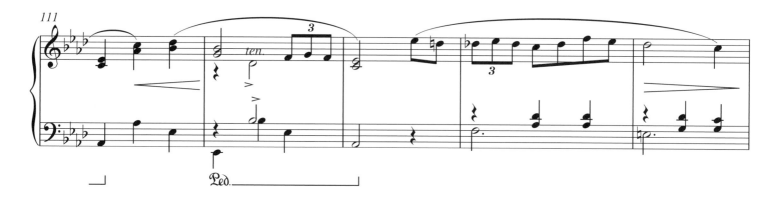

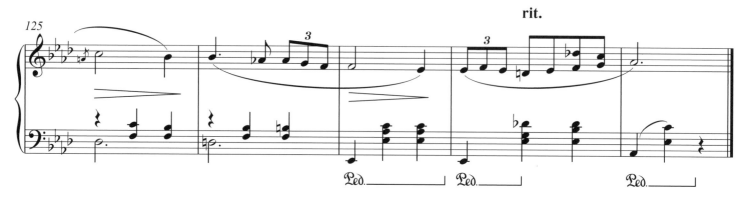

Valse in B minor, Op.69, No.2
(Posthumous)

Composed by Frédéric Chopin

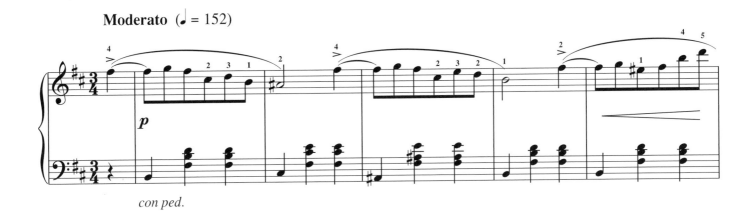

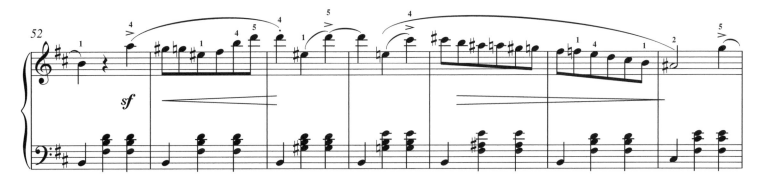

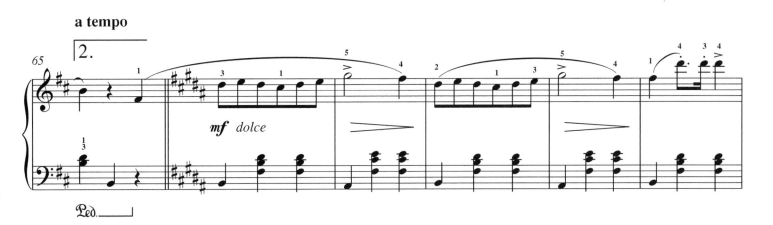

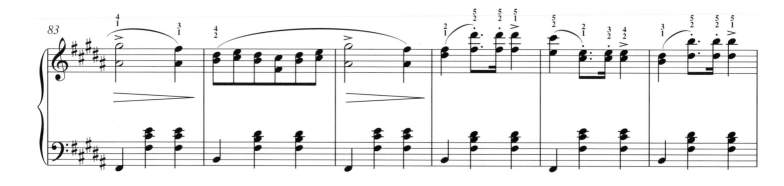

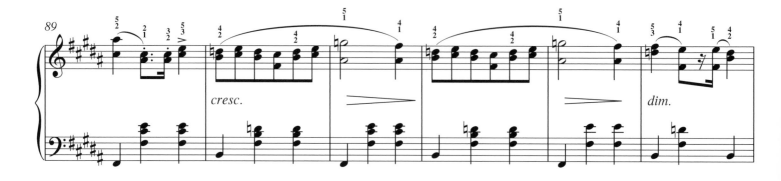

94

poco rall.   a tempo

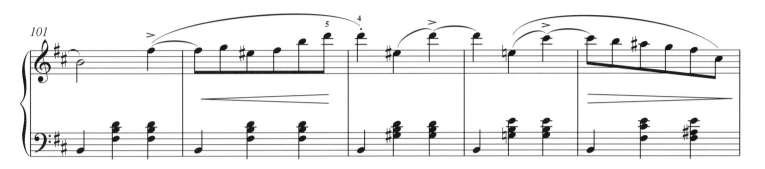

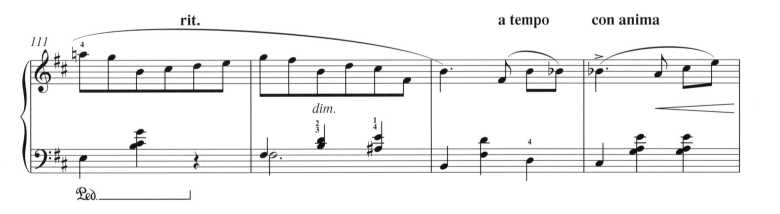

rit.   a tempo   con anima

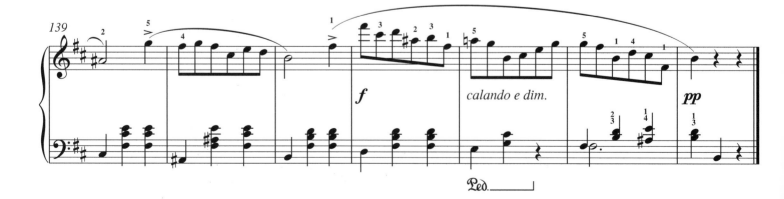

123456789